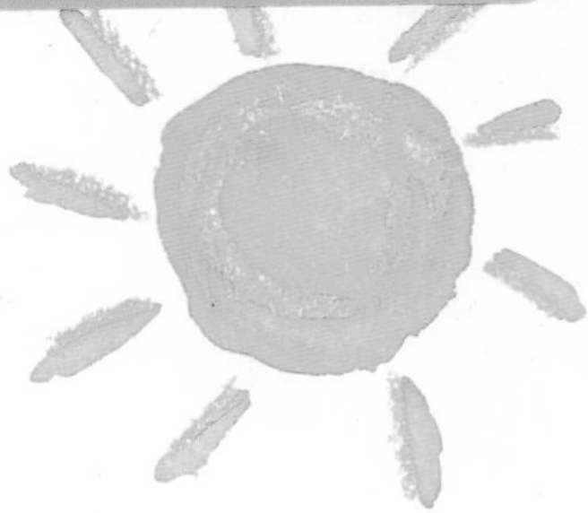

This is the sun.

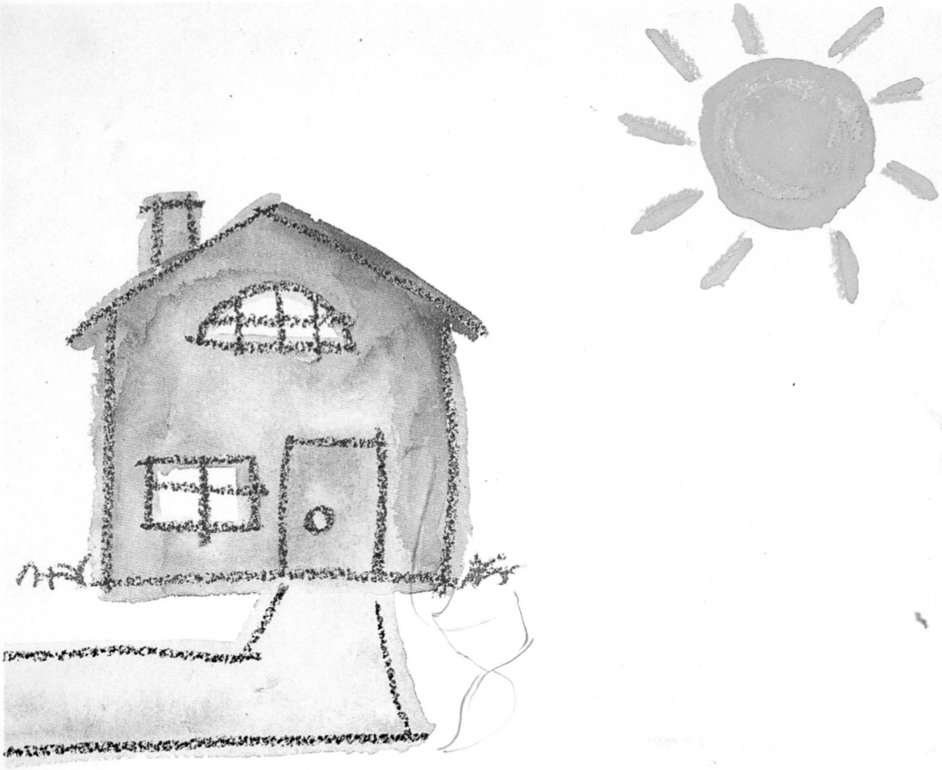

This is a house.

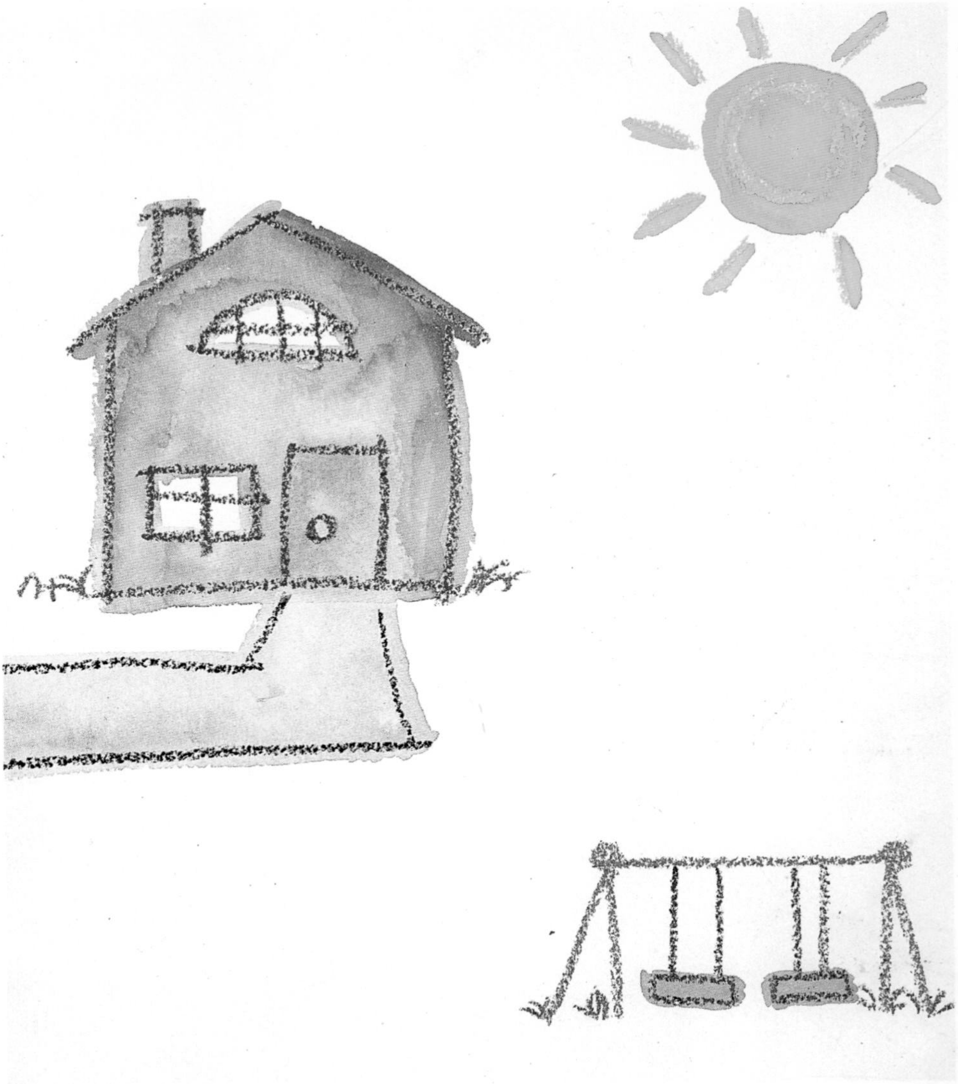

This is a swing set.

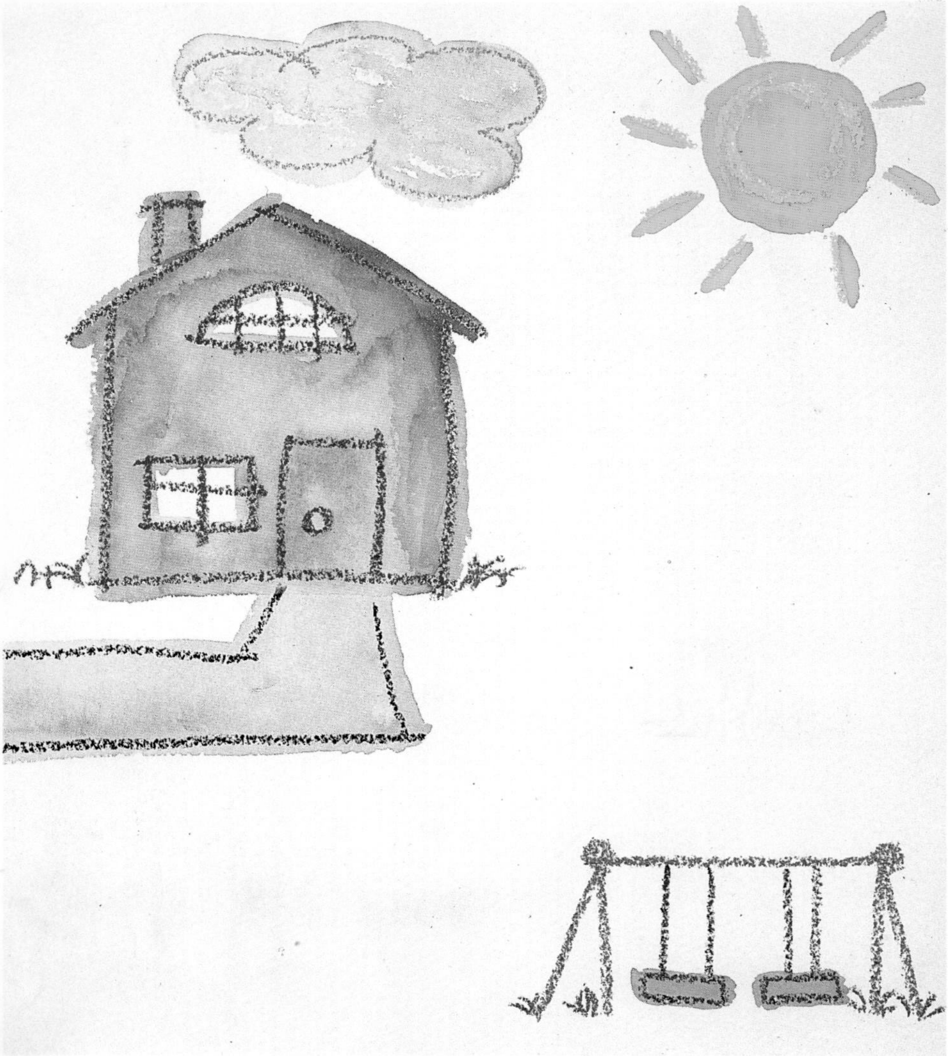

This is a cloud.

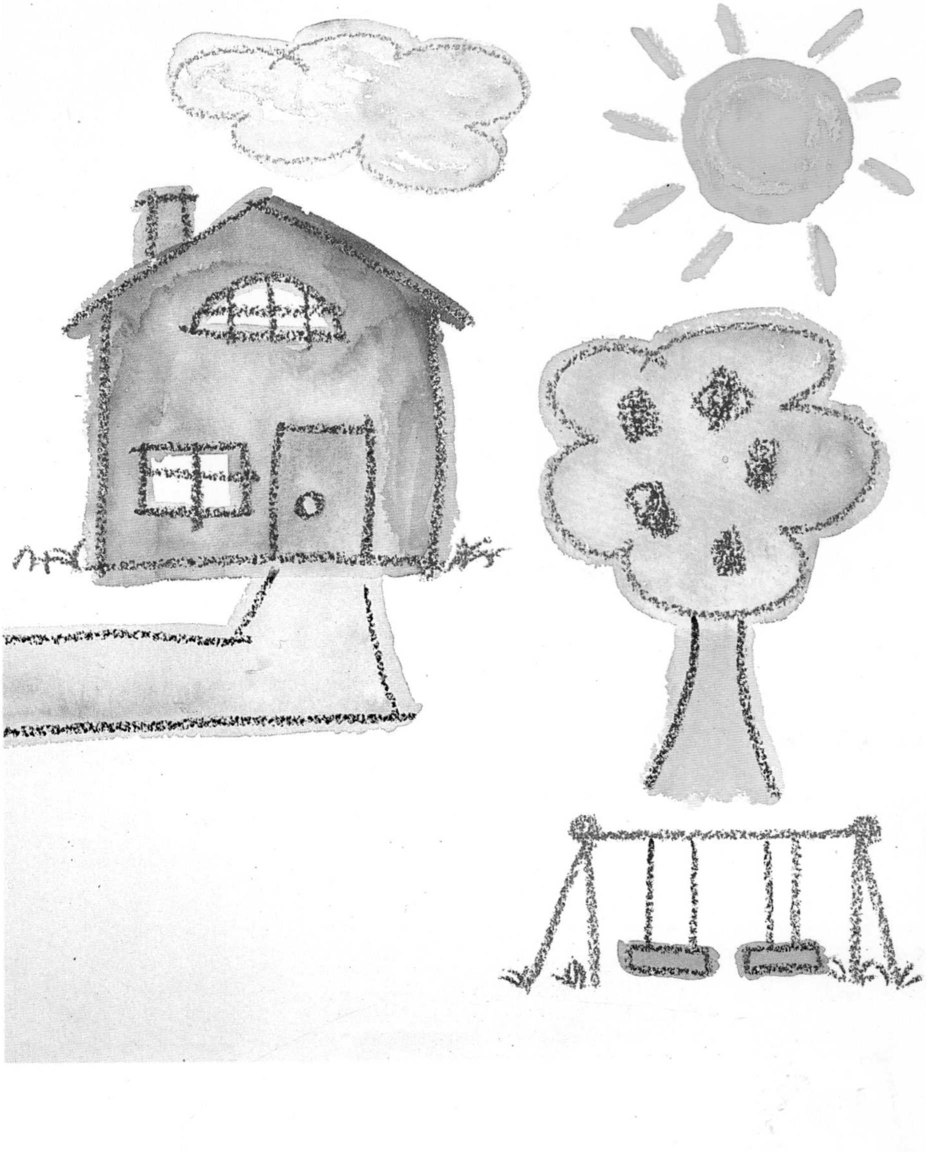

Here is a tree.

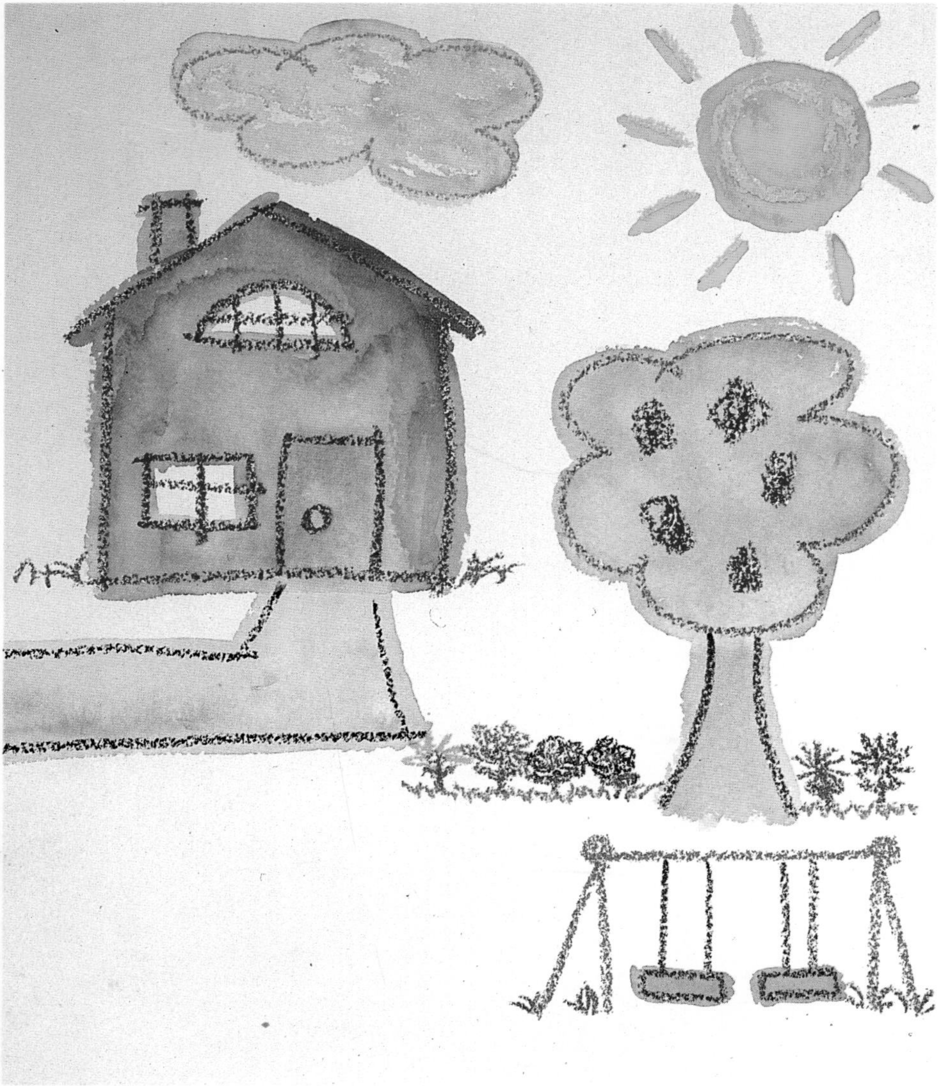

Here are some flowers.

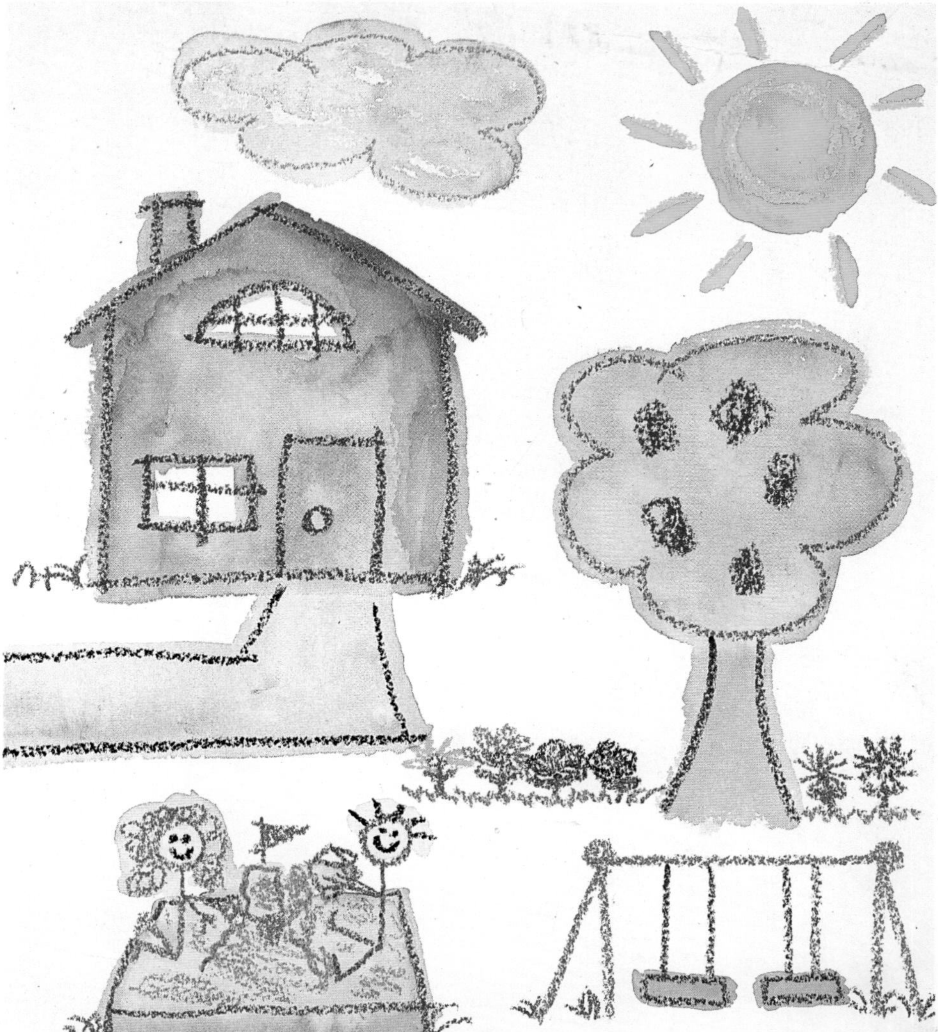

Here are some children playing in the sandbox.

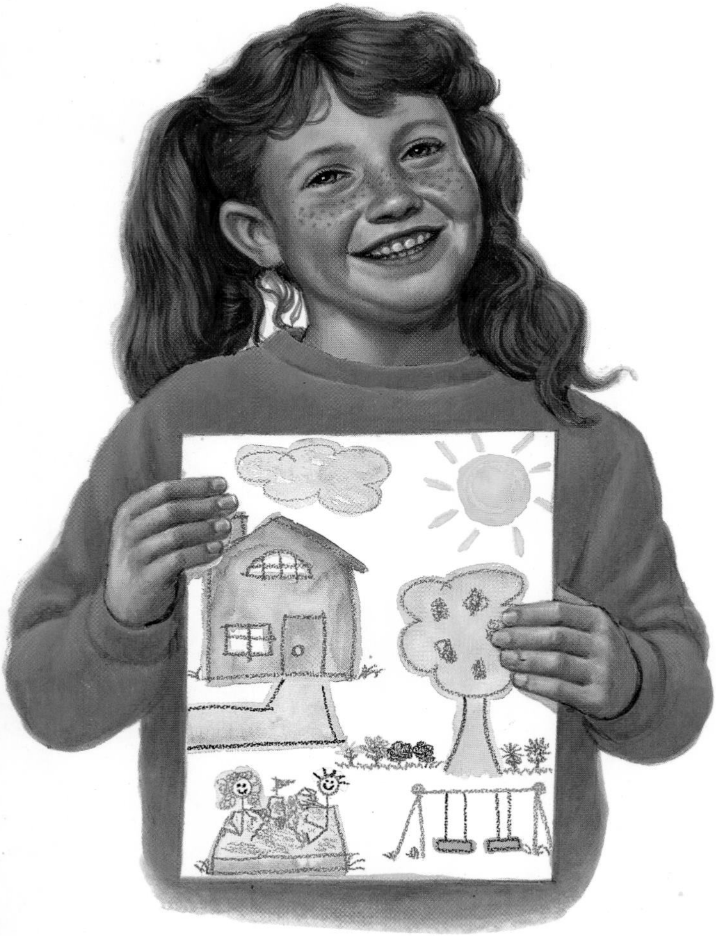

I drew this picture.